CountryMu★S
KEITH URBAN

By Ruben Hakit

Gareth Stevens
Publishing

Please visit our Web site www.garethstevens.com. For a free color catalog of all our high-quality books, call toll free 1-800-542-2595 or fax 1-877-542-2596.

Library of Congress Cataloging-in-Publication Data

Hakit, Ruben.
  Keith Urban / Ruben Hakit.
      p. cm. — (Country music stars)
  Includes bibliographical references and index.
  ISBN 978-1-4339-3605-0 (pbk.)
  ISBN 978-1-4339-3606-7 (6-pack)
  ISBN 978-1-4339-3604-3 (library binding)
  1. Urban, Keith, 1967—Juvenile literature. 2. Country musicians—Australia—Biography—Juvenile literature. I. Title.
  ML3930.U83H35 2010
  782.421642092—dc22

[B]

2009040603

Published in 2010 by Gareth Stevens Publishing
111 East 14th Street, Suite 349
New York, NY 10003

Copyright © 2010 Gareth Stevens Publishing

Designer: Daniel Hosek
Editor: Greg Roza

Photo credits: Cover (background) Shutterstock.com; cover (Urban), title page, p. 17 © Larry Busacca/Getty Images; p. 5 © Stephen Lovekin/Getty Images; pp. 7, 15 © Paul Natkin/WireImage/Getty Images; p. 9 © Ethan Miller/Getty Images; p. 11 © Jason Merritt/Getty Images; p. 13 © M. Caulfield/WireImage/Getty Images; p. 19 © Frank Micelotta/Getty Images; p. 21 © Archie Carpenter/Getty Images; p. 23 © Dan MacMedan/WireImage/Getty Images; p. 25 © Fotonoticias/WireImage/Getty Images; p. 27 © Lorenzo Santini/FilmMagic/Getty Images; p. 29 © Kevin Mazur/WireImage/Getty Images.

Printed in the United States of America

CPSIA compliance information: Batch #CW10GS: For further information contact Gareth Stevens, New York, New York at 1-800-542-2595.

CONTENTS

GUITAR STAR

Keith Urban is a country music singer and more. He also writes songs and plays the guitar.

NATURAL TALENT

Keith was born in New Zealand in 1967. His family moved to Australia when he was very young.

Keith began taking guitar lessons when he was 6.

Keith began winning singing contests when he was 8.

Keith's dad listened to American country music while Keith was growing up. Keith started playing country music.

MAKING MUSIC

Keith made his first country album
in 1991. It sold well in Australia and
New Zealand.

Keith moved to Nashville, Tennessee, in 1992. Nashville is the center of American country music.

Keith formed a band. He named it
The Ranch. They made an album
in 1997.

19

Keith made his first solo album in 1999. He has written many hit singles since then.

21

AWARD WINNER

Keith has been winning music awards all his life. He won Grammys in 2006 and 2008!

MEET KEITH'S FAMILY

Keith is married to a famous actress from Australia. Her name is Nicole Kidman.

AUSTRA

25

Keith and Nicole have a daughter named Sunday Rose. She was born in July 2008.

KEITH'S FANS

Keith is one of the hottest country stars today. He has many fans.

29

TIMELINE

1967 Keith Urban is born in New Zealand.

1991 Keith makes his first album.

1992 Keith moves to Nashville, Tennessee.

1997 The Ranch puts out an album.

1999 Keith makes his first solo album.

2006 Keith wins his first Grammy.

2006 Keith gets married to Nicole Kidman.

2008 Keith wins his second Grammy.

2008 Keith's daughter Sunday Rose is born.

FOR MORE INFORMATION

Books:

Leavitt, Amie Jane. *Keith Urban*. Hockessin, DE: Mitchell Lane Publishers, 2008.

Riggs, Kate. *Country Music*. Mankato, MN: Creative Education, 2008.

Web Sites:

Keith Urban
www.keithurban.net

CMT: Keith Urban
www.cmt.com/artists/az/urban_keith/artist.jhtml

GLOSSARY

award: a prize given to someone for doing something well

contest: an event in which two or more people try to win a prize

Grammy: an American award given each year to a musician

hit single: a song that is played a lot and liked by many people

solo album: an album put out by a single musician, rather than a group of musicians

INDEX